Area 51 Alien and UFO Mysteries

by Carol Kim

CAPSTONE PRESS
a capstone imprint

Published by Capstone Press, an imprint of Capstone
1710 Roe Crest Drive, North Mankato, Minnesota 56003
capstonepub.com

Library of Congress Cataloging-in-Publication Data
Title: Area 51 alien and UFO mysteries / by Carol Kim.
Description: North Mankato, Minnesota : Capstone Press, an imprint of Capstone, [2022] | Series: History's mysteries | Includes bibliographical references and index. | Audience: Ages 8-11 | Audience: Grades 4-6 | Summary: "A highly secure military base sits in the middle of the Nevada desert. What happens inside is kept top secret. Many UFO sightings have been reported nearby. Some people even say alien bodies are stored there. What really goes on behind its highly guarded fences? Explore the theories and learn why Area 51 has become one of history's greatest mysteries"-- Provided by publisher.
Identifiers: LCCN 2021027882 (print) | LCCN 2021027883 (ebook) | ISBN 9781663958785 (hardcover) | ISBN 9781666320855 (paperback) | ISBN 9781666320862 (pdf) | ISBN 9781666320886 (kindle edition)
Subjects: LCSH: Area 51 (Nev.)--Juvenile literature. | Air bases--Nevada--Juvenile literature. | Unidentified flying objects--Juvenile literature. | Research aircraft--United States--Juvenile literature. | Official secrets--United States--Juvenile literature.
Classification: LCC UG634.5.A74 K56 2022 (print) | LCC UG634.5.A74 (ebook) | DDC 001.94209793--dc23
LC record available at https://lccn.loc.gov/2021027882
LC ebook record available at https://lccn.loc.gov/2021027883

Editorial Credits
Editor: Carrie Sheely; Designer: Kim Pfeffer; Media Researcher: Morgan Walters; Production Specialist: Laura Manthe

Image Credits
Alamy: AF archive, 11; Getty Images: DigitalGlobe, 7, gremlin, 28, HIGH-G Productions/Stocktrek Images, 23, Jerod Harris, 15, mj0007, 13; Library of Congress, 8; NASA: Johnson Space Center, 25; Newscom: Gabe Zeifman/Cover-Images, top 19; Shutterstock: Angel DiBilio, 9, CloudOnePhoto, 5, Dabarti CGI, 27, Dylan. King, 6, Eliyahu Yosef Parypa, bottom 19, Jose Gil, 10, Keith Tarrier, 21, Logan Bush, 22, Melkor3D, Cover, Ursatii, 17; Wikimedia: Courtesy, Fort Worth Star-Telegram Photograph Collection, Special Collections, The University of Texas at Arlington Library, Arlington, Texas, 16

All internet sites appearing in back matter were available and accurate when this book was sent to press.

Table of Contents

Words in **bold** are in the glossary.

INTRODUCTION

Do Not Enter!

Driving along the lonely road known as the **Extraterrestrial** Highway in Nevada, there's not much to see besides desert—until the road ends. Here, drivers find signs reading *Off-Limits* and *No Trespassing*. Those who choose to ignore the signs run the risk of being arrested. Cameras watch their every move. Guards sit in trucks, ready to swoop in and stop anyone who would dare to enter.

Why have the travelers been stopped? They have reached Area 51, part of a U.S. military base. Top-secret government work has taken place there since the 1950s. For years, people have reported seeing many **Unidentified Flying Objects** (UFOs) around Area 51. Because of the reports, some people believe work involving UFOs and **aliens** takes place at Area 51. Could this be true? What goes on in this patch of land in Nevada's desert is a great mystery.

A sign tells travelers that they cannot go into Area 51.

Fact

Everyone who works at Area 51 must have top-secret government clearance. Workers are also told not to talk about their work, not even to their families.

CHAPTER 1

What Is Area 51?

For years, Area 51 was so secret that the government refused to say it existed. It is located near Groom Lake within the 2.9-million-acre (1.1-million-hectare) Nevada Test and Training Range. It is part of Nellis Air Force Base. Area 51 is completely closed to the public. It is even illegal to fly over Area 51.

The entrance to Area 51

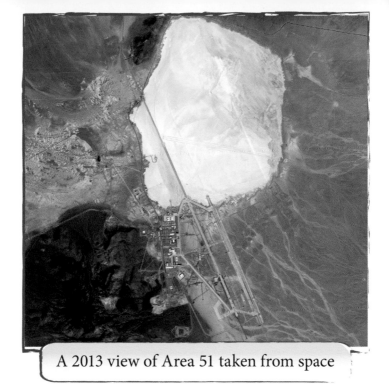

A 2013 view of Area 51 taken from space

In the late 1800s, the area was mined for silver and lead. Later, the U.S. government used the area to test new planes. In the 1950s, the government began exploding **nuclear** weapons for testing at the Nevada Test Site next to Area 51.

NOT EXACTLY PARADISE

In the early days, Area 51 was called Paradise Ranch. Getting people to take a job in the middle of the desert was hard. Making it sound like a resort was a way to attract workers. The government even hired professional chefs from Las Vegas to provide fancy meals to employees. At different times it had other nicknames, including Dreamland, Watertown, and Yuletide.

Super Spy Planes

In 1954, President Dwight D. Eisenhower wanted a secret place for the military. He wanted to develop spy planes to check on the Soviet Union's weapons program. This was during the Cold War. It was a time when U.S. and Soviet Union rivalry was at its peak after World War II (1939–1945).

Dwight D. Eisenhower

Beginning in 1955, the Air Force tested spy planes at Area 51. The first plane built was the U-2. It could fly at a height of 70,000 feet (21,336 meters). This was much higher than any other planes at the time. It could take detailed photos of the ground even while flying almost 13 miles (21 kilometers) high.

The U-2 has been in service nearly 70 years.

Next, the government began working on the A-12. It made its first flight in 1962. The A-12 could fly close to 2,200 miles (3,541 km) per hour. It could take photos 90,000 feet (27,432 m) above the ground.

If the work done at Area 51 is secret, how is so much known about these aircraft projects? In 2013, the U.S. government released documents about the history of the U-2 and A-12 spy planes. They proved that Area 51 existed.

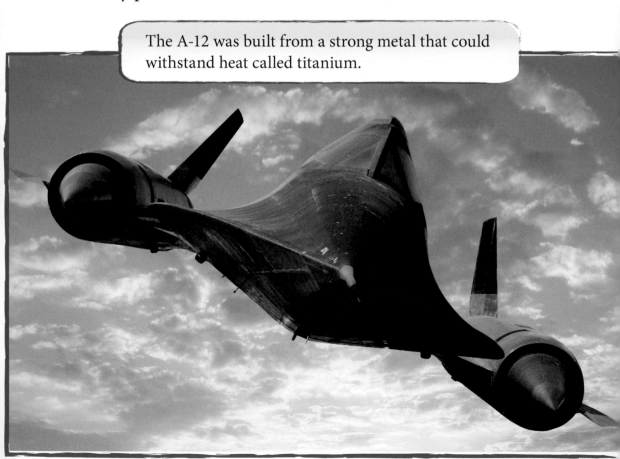

The A-12 was built from a strong metal that could withstand heat called titanium.

Today, the government continues to be very secretive about Area 51. Are officials trying to hide something?

Fact

Area 51 has found its way into many movies and TV shows. It was a part of the 1996 movie *Independence Day*. Area 51 has also been included in the *X-Files* TV series and *The Simpsons*.

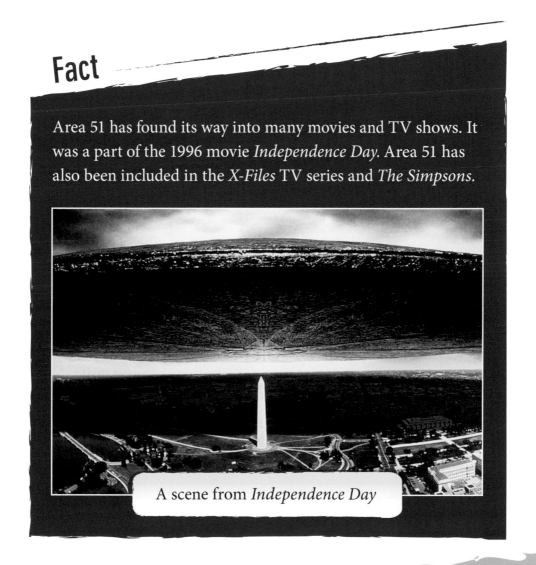

A scene from *Independence Day*

CHAPTER 2

Is the Government Hiding Alien Secrets?

Some people think work on UFOs and aliens takes place at Area 51. This idea began in 1947. A rancher discovered a mysterious object that had crashed near Roswell, New Mexico. Newspapers called the object a flying disk. The Air Force later said the crashed object was a weather balloon. Many people did not believe this report. Rumors began to grow that the government was trying to cover up what happened. People said Air Force officials took the object for study. Some people said bodies of aliens from the crashed object were later brought to Area 51.

The connection between Area 51 and UFOs increased in the 1950s. People reported many UFOs around Area 51. Some reports came from airline pilots. They said they saw fiery disks and flying saucers. These aircraft were flying much higher than what was believed to be possible.

Disc-shaped objects were one type of UFO reported near Roswell.

Truth or Lies?

The link between UFOs and Area 51 gained more attention in 1989. A man named Bob Lazar was interviewed by a Las Vegas TV station. He said he had worked at Area 51 studying a flying saucer. He believed it was an alien aircraft. He also reported he had seen a body of an alien-like creature.

Many people did not believe Lazar. The government said he had never worked at Area 51. Lazar appeared to have lied about his education. The schools showed no record of him going there. But others think Lazar was telling the truth. He knew details about Area 51 that were not publicly known. One reporter found other people to back up parts of Lazar's story. The attention given to Lazar's story pushed Area 51 into the spotlight.

Bob Lazar answered questions during a screening of the documentary *Bob Lazar: Area 51 and Flying Saucers* in 2018.

A Strange Material

Later, new information about Roswell came out. In 1994, the Air Force released a report. It again said the crashed object was a balloon. Sensors and other equipment were included in the debris. The gear was part of a program called Project Mogul.

In 2007, the son of Major Jesse Marcel, who had investigated the original crash, shared his father's story. He said his father had been told to keep quiet about the crash. He said his father described the debris material as not from Earth. The story renewed people's interest in UFOs and Roswell.

Major Jesse Marcel holds debris from the Roswell crash in 1947.

More Government Explanations

The government said it could explain the UFO sightings near Area 51. According to a 1997 article in a Central Intelligence Agency (CIA) journal, the U-2 and SR-71 spy planes were the reason for most of the UFO reports. To some, this made sense. The very high speeds and flying altitudes of the planes could have made them seem to be from another world. Light could have reflected off the aircraft material in ways that made it appear shiny or fiery.

In 2013, the CIA officially said Area 51 existed. But the government has not been able to explain all of the UFO sightings.

Although people study UFO reports, many of them remain unexplained.

Just a Secret Military Base

By the mid-1970s, the government wondered whether it needed to continue using Area 51. It was no longer necessary to practice flying U-2 and A-12 spy planes there. But Air Force officials decided they needed Area 51. They wanted to keep making new **technology** and aircraft.

There may be nothing mysterious happening at Area 51. The government could just be creating cutting-edge equipment and aircraft to protect the United States.

The secret activities at Area 51 could have nothing to do with aliens or alien spacecraft.

TOP-SECRET COMMUTE

Much about Area 51 is unusual, including how people travel there for work. Employees fly in and out on unmarked planes from McCarran International Airport in Las Vegas. The airline is known as Janet Airlines. The planes fly out of their own **terminal** at McCarran. Some say Janet stands for Just Another Non-Existent Terminal. But it could stand for Joint Air Network for Employee Transportation.

A plane from Janet Airlines takes off from McCarran airport.

More Spy Planes

Some clues give peeks into what is taking place at Area 51. According to government-released information, a number of **stealth** projects continued to be developed and tested at Area 51 after the 1970s. They included aircraft designed to stay hidden from enemy **radar**. The SR-71 Blackbird was one of these planes. The SR-71 flew 2,193 miles (3,529 km) per hour. It was retired in 1990 and remains one of the world's fastest aircraft.

There are rumors of other aircraft that may have been tested at Area 51. One could fly at speeds of Mach 5, or more than 3,800 miles (6,116 km) per hour. Another is a small plane that could be flown in space.

The SR-71 Blackbird could fly more than 85,000 feet (25,908 m) above the ground.

Smaller and Stealthier

Area 51 appears to still be in use. **Satellite** images show the facility has grown since the 1960s. But it is believed most of the work is done underground, hidden from overhead view.

Fact

Tourists visit the nearby town of Rachel, Nevada, to enjoy the UFO and alien-themed attractions. There is a restaurant called the Little A'Le'Inn with alien burgers on the menu.

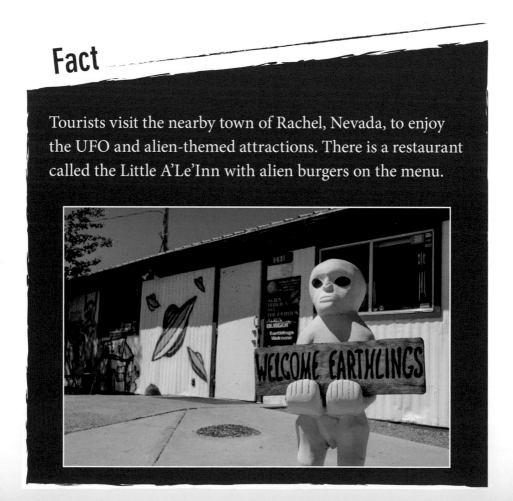

What is the government using Area 51 for now? Many believe the focus has shifted toward developing and testing unmanned aerial vehicles (UAVs). These are sometimes known as drones. Drones are flown by remote control. They make it possible to fight in battles without putting troops in danger.

The Predator and Reaper drones are known to be connected with Area 51. The Predator was in service until 2018. It had cameras that could provide clear images from a distance. The MQ-1 version carried weapons. The newer Reaper has the ability to carry more weapons than the MQ-1.

An MQ-9 Reaper flies on a training mission.

CHAPTER 4

Other Secret Activities

Secrecy surrounds Area 51. This leads some people to connect Area 51 with ideas other than aliens and UFOs. Many are far-fetched. Most people think they are untrue.

Fake Lunar Landing

The author of a book published in 1974 claimed the Apollo moon landing in 1969 was filmed on a movie set located at Area 51. Some people believed him. It's true that astronauts had visited the Nevada Test Site next to Area 51 to practice walking and driving on a moon-like surface. Underground bomb tests done at the Nevada site had created craters on the ground like those on the moon. But evidence overwhelmingly shows the lunar landing took place.

A NASA photograph shows astronaut Edwin Aldrin Jr. on the moon during the 1969 Apollo mission.

Huge Underground Railroad System

Some people say Area 51 has a big underground railroad system. The underground system supposedly connects military and other secret facilities all across the country. Former Area 51 workers have said Area 51 does have underground tunnels, but not a huge underground railway network.

Weather Experiments

Some people believe there were efforts to create storms that could be used as weapons against enemy countries at Area 51. Scientists have experimented with making clouds to produce rain. But this work was aimed at helping farmers, not creating weapons.

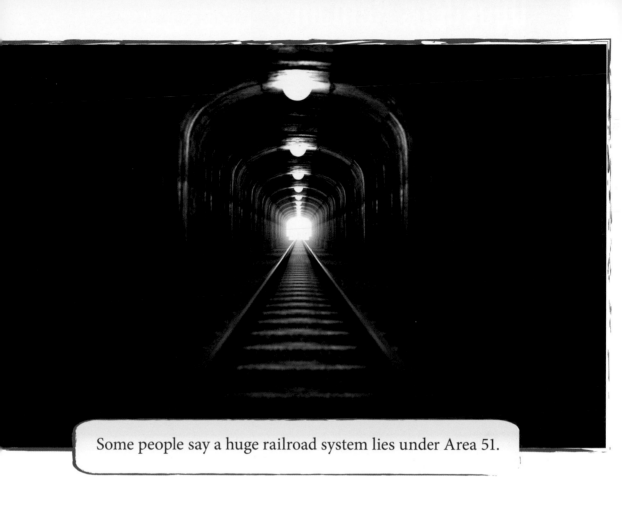

Some people say a huge railroad system lies under Area 51.

Fact

Some people have suggested that time-travel studies are conducted at Area 51.

Questions Remain

Although we know Area 51 is real, many questions remain about what kind of work is going on there. The secrecy leads people to imagine a variety of ideas.

It is known the government has tested spy planes and weapons at Area 51. Is that the only kind of work being done there? Or could the reports of UFOs and aliens be true? Is the government hiding other activities? We may not ever know exactly what goes on at Area 51.

An artist's idea of what secret studies of UFOs might look like

The Main Theories

1. The Government Is Hiding UFOs and Aliens

Many do not believe the government's explanation that what crashed in Roswell, New Mexico, was a spy balloon. Bob Lazar described working on alien spacecraft at Area 51. Could the government have taken a spacecraft and alien bodies to Area 51 to study? The government claims it can explain most of the UFO sightings that have been reported by the public. But what about the ones that are not explained?

2. Only Top-Secret Technology Is Built and Tested

The government was forced to reveal information about spy planes that were tested at Area 51 in the 1950s and 1960s. Information about additional stealth planes and weapons have also been released. It makes sense for the government to keep new weapons technology a secret to protect the U.S. from enemies. Could this be the only reason for the intense secrecy?

3. Keeping Other Information From the Public

With so much secrecy surrounding Area 51, many wonder what the government is trying to hide. Could it be keeping information that is not alien-related a secret?

Glossary

alien (AY-lee-uhn)—a being from another planet

altitude (AL-ti-tood)—the height of something above ground or above sea-level

debris (duh-BREE)—the scattered pieces of something that has been broken or destroyed

extraterrestrial (ek-struh-tuh-RESS-tree-uhl)—coming from a place beyond the Earth or our solar system

nuclear (NOO-klee-ur)—having to do with the energy created by splitting atoms; nuclear weapons use this energy to cause an explosion

radar (RAY-dar)—a device that uses radio waves to track the location of objects

satellite (SAT-uh-lite)— a spacecraft that circles Earth; satellites gather and send information to Earth

stealth (STELTH)— having the ability to move secretly

technology (tek-NOL-uh-jee)—the use of science to do practical things, such as designing complex machines

terminal (TUR-mi-nul)—the part of an airport that certain airlines use

UFO—short for Unidentified Flying Object

Read More

Manzanero, Paula K. *Where Is Area 51?* New York: Penguin Workshop, 2018.

Steinkraus, Kyla. *Area 51.* North Mankato, MN: Black Rabbit Books, 2017.

Zalewski, Aubrey. *Area 51.* North Mankato, MN: Capstone, 2020.

Internet Sites

Britannica Kids: Roswell Incident
kids.britannica.com/students/article/Roswell-Incident/313285

CBC Kids: What Exactly Are UFOs?
cbc.ca/kidscbc2/the-feed/what-exactly-are-ufos

UFO Stories
history.com/ufo-stories

Index

Author Biography

Carol Kim is the author of several fiction and nonfiction books for kids. She enjoys researching and uncovering little-known facts and sharing what she learns with young readers. Carol lives in Austin, Texas, with her family. Learn more about her and her latest books at her website, CarolKimBooks.com.